HOW TO LOOK AFTER YOUR

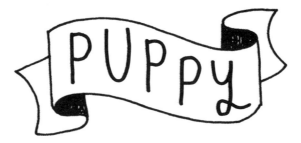

PUPPY

WIDE EYED EDITIONS

Wide Eyed Editions
www.wideeyededitions.com

How To Look After Your Puppy © Aurum Press Ltd 2015
Text © Helen Piers Estate 2015

First published in the United States in 2015 by Wide Eyed Editions
an imprint of Quarto Inc.,
276 Fifth Avenue, Suite 206, New York, NY 10001.
www.wideeyededitions.com

ISBN 978-1-84780-699-4

The illustrations were created digitally.
Set in Fugue, A Thousand Years, First Time in Forever and Sue Ellen Francisco

Designed by Nicola Price
Edited by Emily Hawkins and Jenny Broom
Published by Rachel Williams

Printed in Shenzhen, Guangdong, China

1 3 5 7 9 8 6 4 2

CONTENTS

PUPPIES AND DOGS AS PETS

You could not choose a more intelligent and affectionate pet than a dog. Dogs were first domesticated over five thousand years ago, and they have lived as close companions to humans ever since.

Before adopting a puppy it is important to think about what caring for a dog involves and to be quite sure you can give it the kind of life it needs.

THERE ARE SOME THINGS YOU NEED TO THINK ABOUT BEFORE YOU ADOPT A PUPPY...

Will your dog get enough exercise?

Is there a field or park nearby where it's safe to let a dog off the leash to run around?

Can you afford to care for a dog?

You will need to pay for its food and vaccinations, plus any vet's fees if it needs to be spayed or neutered or gets sick.

Will you have the time?

You will need to feed your dog twice a day (or four times a day while it's a puppy), train it, and take it for walks.

Will your dog be left alone too much?

A dog can be left alone for a few hours, but if it's by itself all day it will get lonely and very unhappy. If everyone in your family spends their day at work or school, it would not be kind to keep a dog.

What will you do during vacations?

Will somebody look after the dog for you? Dogs can stay at kennels or with dog-boarding families, but it is expensive.

THE RIGHT DOG FOR YOU

Dogs vary a lot in size, character, and how much exercise they need, so it's important to choose the right kind of dog for you and your home.

This will depend on whether you live in the city or country, how much time you have to exercise and groom your dog, and how large a dog you can handle. Another thing to consider is whether there are very young children in your family. Some breeds, like Labradors, are more patient with youngsters than others.

A puppy or an adult?

If this is your first dog, it is best to get a puppy. Adopting a stray adult dog from an animal shelter and giving it a good home is doing it a great kindness, and it might turn out to be a faithful, well-trained dog. On the other hand, it might have been treated cruelly in the past and may have bad habits that are difficult to break, in which case handling it would need skill and experience.

Male or female?

Both make equally good, affectionate pets, although male dogs tend to be more independent, if they have not yet been neutered (see page 30).

PEDIGREE, CROSS-BREED, OR MUTT?

Pedigrees and cross-breeds

A pedigree or pure-bred dog is one whose ancestors were all the same breed. A cross-breed is one whose mother was one breed and its father another.

Pedigree puppies are expensive to buy, but the advantage of getting a pedigree (or a cross-breed, to some extent) is that you have a good idea what it will be like when it's fully grown.

Mutts

The ancestry of a mutt—or mongrel—is very mixed, and usually unknown. It is sometimes hard to tell how big a mixed breed puppy will grow, how energetic and noisy it will be, and whether or not it will be easy to train.

However, mutts make just as good pets as pedigrees and many people prefer them. They tend to be healthier than many pedigree dogs and are cheaper to buy.

DIFFERENT BREEDS OF DOG

There are over a hundred different dog breeds!

Many types of dog were originally bred to do a particular kind of work, and this shows in their characters. Hounds (used for hunting) and working dogs (trained to herd farm animals) all need a lot of space. Terriers (bred to chase prey through burrows) and sporting dogs (trained to bring back game birds shot down by their masters) are faithful and obedient. Other breeds, such as the Tibetan Terrier or the Cavalier King Charles Spaniel, were bred as pets and companions. There are also miniature breeds, which are often too delicate for much roughhousing.

THINGS TO THINK ABOUT WHEN CONSIDERING DIFFERENT BREEDS

- How big do they grow?
- How much exercise do they need?
- If you live in a city, do they adapt well to city life?
- Do they need a lot of grooming?
- Are they likely to be aggressive toward other dogs or strangers?
- How easy are they to train?
- Are they quiet, or do they bark a lot?

Tibetan Terrier

Size: Small/medium
Type: Companion
* Very healthy, affectionate, good-natured
* Needs daily brushing

Beagle

Size: Medium
Type: Hound
* Cheerful, very healthy, good with other pets
* Needs careful training or will wander

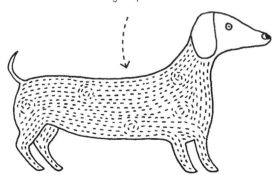

Cavalier King Charles Spaniel

Size: Small
Type: Companion
* Good-natured, clean, cheerful, obedient
* Needs regular grooming

Dachshund

Size: Small
Type: Hound
* Loyal, affectionate, sense of fun
* Prone to back injury, so must not be allowed to put on weight; must be trained not to jump on furniture

Labrador

Size: Medium
Type: Sporting dog
* Affectionate, faithful, trustworthy
* Needs lots of exercise or puts on weight

GETTING READY FOR YOUR PUPPY

Your new puppy will settle in more quickly if everything is ready for it before you bring it home.

Until the puppy is house-trained, you may want to keep it in one room for most of the time. It should be a warm room, near the family, with a floor that is easy to wash.

The puppy will need a bed in a warm corner, not too close to a boiler or radiator. Line the bed with newspaper and a blanket. Remember, if you buy a bed that fits your puppy now, it will soon be too small! A cardboard box will make a cozy bed until you can see how big your puppy will grow.

Puppies chew anything they can get their teeth into! Make sure there are no electric cords around, or anything else they might hurt themselves on.

Make sure your puppy cannot get out of your yard—especially onto a road. You may also need to temporarily put wire netting around any ponds.

YOUR PUPPY WILL NEED...

Food bowl

Water bowl

Grooming supplies

DOG

Toys
for it to chew
on safely

Lots of newspaper
to use when
house-training

DAILY NEWS

CHOOSING A PUPPY

If you want a pedigree puppy, you can search the Kennel Club online, register for local breeders, and look in dog magazines.

Make sure you see the puppies with their mother before you make a choice; this will give you an idea of how they will look and behave when full-grown. To find a cross- or mixed-breed, talk to friends with dogs, or ask at a vet or reputable rescue shelter. Take time to choose your puppy and remember that looks aren't everything: a puppy that comes to you fearlessly and wants to play is a better choice than one who runs away and hides, however good-looking it is! It is usual to choose a puppy when it is a few weeks old, then leave it with its mother until it is about two months.

THERE ARE SOME IMPORTANT QUESTIONS TO ASK WHEN CHOOSING A PUPPY...

🐾 Is it healthy?

A healthy puppy should be alert and ready to play. It should have clear, bright eyes (not bloodshot or runny) and a clean coat with no bare or sore patches. Its ears should be clean without waxy deposits inside, and there should be no sign of diarrhea (dirt around the tail).

🐾 Does it have a pedigree certificate?

If the puppy is pure-bred, you should be given a certificate stating its date of birth and ancestry.

🐾 How old is it?

Between eight and twelve weeks is best. By then the puppy will be independent enough to leave its mother.

🐾 What food is it used to?

Also ask how much it is fed and how often. You should stick with the same diet at first (see pages 18–19).

🐾 Has it been vaccinated?

If it has, the breeder or original owner should give you a certificate. If not, have it vaccinated as soon as possible (see page 28).

🐾 Has it been treated for parasites?

If not, speak to your vet right away.

🐾 Is it partly house-trained?

Also, if your house is noisy and busy, make sure the puppy is used to a similar environment, so it will fit well into your family.

TAKING YOUR PUPPY HOME

The journey

You will need a dog carrier to bring your puppy home. Make it comfortable by lining it with a towel, which will help soak up any little accidents on the way. Ask the driver to go as smoothly as possible, because the puppy may get carsick. On a long journey, you will need to stop occasionally to give him a drink and perhaps some food.

 Remember that until your puppy has had his vaccinations, it is not safe to let him walk in the street, where he might pick up an infection from other dogs.

Welcome home!

When you get home, show the puppy his bed, give him something to eat and a drink of water, then let him explore the room quietly. Puppies need to sleep a lot, so don't overtire him by playing with him too much.

Settling in

If the weather is good you can take your puppy into the yard, but don't leave him out there alone for the first few days, as there may be dangers you hadn't predicted. Be careful how you introduce the new puppy to other pets. Make a fuss of your older cats or dogs when you first show them the puppy, so they don't feel neglected. You should never leave them alone with the puppy while he's small.

A warm hot-water bottle and a ticking clock might help the puppy feel secure.

The first night

Decide right away whether your puppy will sleep in your bedroom, outside in the hall, or on his own. Remember, if he gets used to spending the night in your room while he is young, it will be very difficult to break the habit when he is older. Puppies often cry during the first night because they miss their mother. Try not to go to your puppy every time he whimpers, or he will come to expect this. Instead, you can call some comforting words from the next room. To keep your puppy from feeling lonely, try wrapping a warm hot-water bottle and a ticking clock in a towel, then tucking them in his bed. These will mimic the warmth and heartbeat of the puppy's mother.

 After the first night or two your puppy will feel more confident and should settle down without crying.

HOUSE-TRAINING YOUR PUPPY

Puppies can be house-trained without too much trouble, but you must be patient and not expect your puppy to understand at once. If he makes a mess in the wrong place he is not trying to be naughty, he just doesn't know any better.

Starting out

First, teach your puppy to use newspaper spread out on the floor. Whenever he looks as if he wants to go—he will probably whimper, turn in circles and sniff the floor —lift him up, take him to the newspaper, and gently hold him there until he has finished. Then praise and make a big fuss

over him. Decide on a word to use when your puppy goes to the bathroom. Always use the same word and he will soon recognize it and know what you want. When you replace the wet newspaper, leave a small piece behind so the smell will encourage him to come back and use it next time.

Going outside

You can gradually move the newspapers toward the door, then out into the yard. You may want to set aside a particular spot in your yard as a bathroom area. Start to take your puppy out to the bathroom area first thing in the morning and after his meals. He will begin to sniff at the door and bark when he needs to go out.

You may decide to mark out a bit of your yard as a bathroom area.

Vinegar

Paper towels

Rubber gloves

Accidents happen!

If the puppy makes a mess on the floor, wash the area thoroughly then rinse it with a mixture of water and vinegar (remember to wear rubber gloves). The smell of vinegar will discourage him from using the same place again. If you see the puppy making a mess in the house, pick him up and rush him outside to the bathroom area. If you haven't seen him do it, just clean up the mess—don't punish him or get angry.

FEEDING YOUR PUPPY

If you weren't given feeding instructions by the breeder or original owner ask your vet for advice.

To avoid upsetting your puppy's stomach, once she is settled on a particular diet you should stick to it, unless there is a problem or your vet advises you to change. If you do change, do it gradually over ten days. High-quality manufactured puppy food is designed to give puppies all the nutrients they need. It's hard to say exactly how much to give as all dogs are different, but follow the guidelines on the container. You could start by putting down a saucerful at each meal. If she gobbles it all up at once and still seems hungry, you will know she needs more.

Choose a quiet place to feed your puppy. Don't try to play with her or interrupt while she is eating. Clear away any uneaten food once your puppy has finished, but always leave a bowl of fresh water out.

How often should I feed my puppy?

Puppies can burn twice as much energy as adult dogs but have smaller stomachs, so they need to be fed little and often. Try not to feed your puppy immediately before or after exercise.

 Up to 4 months: 4 meals a day

 4–6 months: 3 meals a day

 Over 6 months: 2 meals a day (depending on breed)

What not to feed your puppy

Avoid feeding your puppy scraps from the table, as this will encourage her to beg and may cause her to put on too much weight. You should never feed your dog raw meat, chocolate, onions, or grapes and raisins, which can be very harmful.

Treats and chews

Try not to give your dog too many treats— you may want to save them to use as rewards. Make sure they are healthy, such as small pieces of chicken. Don't give bones to your dog, as they could splinter and cause damage. Instead, you can get her a rawhide chew, which will help keep her teeth healthy.

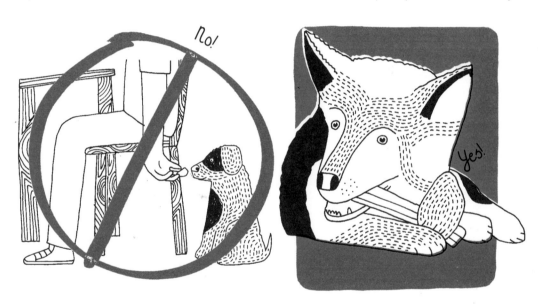

Feeding an adult dog

When your dog is fully grown (usually at about 12–18 months) you can gradually start giving her adult dog food instead of puppy food. Usually, the smaller your dog, the faster it will reach its adult size. Again, choose a high-quality brand of complete dog food suitable for your type of dog—this can be either wet (canned) or dry. You shouldn't leave wet dog food out for more than half an hour, as it might go bad. You should leave a bowl of fresh water out at all times. If you have a medium–sized or large dog, you should use a raised bowl to stop her from gulping down air, which could make her sick.

OBEDIENCE TRAINING

Training a dog takes time and patience, but is well worth the trouble. From an early age, you can teach your dog simple commands, such as "heel," "sit," "stay," and "come."

Collars and leashes

Before training your puppy, he will need to get used to walking on the leash. Your puppy can begin to wear a collar at three months. After a few days, start to attach the leash and walk him around for a few minutes each day. He may not like it at first and might pull and tug. Be firm, but not rough. Persuade him to follow you by praising and coaxing him.

DOG-TRAINING TIPS

 Be kind, but firm.

 Always use the same command words so your dog doesn't get confused.

 Work on only one command at a time.

 Don't use punishment, only praise. At first, you may want to reward your dog with a treat when he gets it right.

 Don't overtire your dog. Ten minutes of training a day is enough.

Walking to "heel"

With the dog close behind you, hold the leash in front of you, with your second hand halfway down it, ready to restrain the dog. The leash should be slack. If the dog drags on it, pull him back and say "heel."

Training to "sit"

With the shortened leash in one hand, gently press down the dog's hindquarters with the other hand, palm flat, as you say "sit." Don't press on his back, except close to the tail, or you may hurt him.

STAY!

Training to "stay"

Face your dog, raise one hand—palm toward him—and say "stay" as you move away a step or two. If he follows, say "no," and begin again. As he gets the idea you can move farther away bit by bit.

Training to "come"

From a short distance away, face your dog, call "come!" and pat your legs. Increase the distance as he understands what you want. When he arrives make a big fuss over him and reward him with a treat.

EXERCISE

Dogs can't stay healthy if they don't get enough exercise.
They also get bored if they are kept inside for too long, so you
should walk your dog at least once a day.

There will be times when you don't feel like taking your dog out, but when you see
how her tail wags when you pick up her leash, it will seem worth it! Dogs have an
amazing sense of smell. For them, half the enjoyment of a run is to explore,
following interesting scents. You can have fun exercising your dog—some love
jumping, others enjoy fetching balls or frisbees. Don't throw sticks though,
because they could splinter in your dog's mouth, causing injuries.

IMPORTANT THINGS TO REMEMBER...

 Keep your dog on a leash in the street,
or in the countryside where
sheep or cattle are grazing.

 Train her to sit while you wait to
cross the road.

 She must wear an ID tag with your
name and address engraved into it.

 Don't let your dog poop on the sidewalk or the
grass in a park. Dog poop contains germs that
can cause people serious illness, so always use
a plastic bag to pick up after your dog and then
put it in a trashcan.

FETCH!

The law and dogs

By law, the owner is responsible for a dog's behavior and may be prosecuted if the dog poops on the sidewalk, causes an accident, attacks a person or another animal, or chases farm animals. It is sensible to take out insurance against possible damage caused by your dog.

HEEL!

ID tags and microchips

It is not good—and in many places it's illegal—to let your dog roam the streets alone, as she could get run over or lost. But she might get out without you knowing, so make sure she has an ID tag on her collar. If your dog ever slips her collar or you let go of her leash by accident, don't chase after her; she will think you are playing and run away from you. Instead, call her and run in the opposite direction— then she will chase YOU! It is a good idea to have your dog microchipped, so if she gets lost (and loses her collar) she can be returned to you.

GAMES TO PLAY WITH YOUR DOG

Dogs love playing with other dogs, people or toys. Outside or inside, you can have some great fun with your puppy.

Hide and seek

Hide in another room or behind a piece of furniture, then call your dog's name. Give him lots of praise when he finds you. You could even hide one of his favorite toys instead of yourself. First, show the dog the toy, then put him somewhere he can't see you while you hide it. Tell him to find the toy, giving him hints along the way. When he finds it, make a big fuss over him.

Which box?

In this game, your dog can play detective using his amazing sense of smell. Place a few containers upside down on the floor. One of them should have a toy or treat hidden underneath. Encourage your dog to investigate the boxes until he pauses at the one with the hidden surprise. Once he knows what's expected, you can add more boxes to make it more of a challenge.

Agility course

Make an agility course using rolled-up blankets or towels. Walk your dog through the course, asking him to hop over the hurdles. Once he is familiar with it, ask him to stay at one end of the course, then call him from the other.

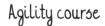

Staircase sprint

If it's yucky weather outside, this is a good way for your dog to burn off some energy, but do NOT play this with dogs under a year old – their joints aren't strong enough to take the impact. Stand at the bottom of the stairs and throw a toy up to the hallway, then let your dog dash upstairs to fetch it.

GROOMING

Grooming your puppy will help her stay clean and healthy.

Regular grooming keeps her coat in good condition, gets rid of dirt and loose hairs, and massages her skin. Start grooming your puppy from a young age so that she learns to enjoy it. At first, use a soft brush and keep the sessions short until she gets used to it. Remember to give her lots of praise!

Long-haired dogs

If your dog is long-haired, you should groom her every day to avoid the hair getting matted. First, use a comb or pinhead brush to tease out the tangles. Finish with a bristle brush to make her coat shine. Always brush and comb the way the hair grows, and be careful not to scratch the skin. You may need to take long- or medium-haired breeds to a professional groomer occasionally for some clipping. Never use scissors on your dog—leave this to the professionals!

Short-haired dogs

Short-haired dogs need only a weekly brushing with a bristle brush, followed by a stroke-down with a rubber grooming glove to remove loose hairs.

Things to check

Grooming your dog gives you a chance to look for lumps, bumps, or scratches that might need to be checked by a vet. You should also make sure that her ears are clean inside, her claws aren't split or growing too long, and that there are no bare patches in her coat.
All of these would need treatment.

Smile!

It is recommended that you brush your dog's teeth twice a week using a special dog toothbrush and toothpaste. You only need to brush the outside surfaces, as your dog will use her tongue to clean the rest.

Your dog may get nervous at bath time, so she will need lots of praise and reassurance.

Bath time

Generally a dog doesn't need bathing more than three or four times a year, but if yours is getting smelly, has rolled in something yucky, or is light-colored, more often can't hurt. You will need to use a shampoo designed for your dog's type of coat. Use lukewarm water, and only run it up to your dog's knees. Wet her coat using either the shower attachment or a container of water, then lather all over, being careful not to get shampoo in her eyes or ears. Rinse carefully, then towel-dry her thoroughly and keep her somewhere warm untill she's completely dry.

KEEPING YOUR DOG HEALTHY

There are a few things you can do to make sure your dog doesn't get sick and to keep her in good condition.

If your dog seems sick, isn't eating, or has diarrhea for more than a few days, make sure you see a vet. Even a dog that seems healthy should see the vet once a year for a check-up and vaccinations.

If your puppy is used to being handled from a young age, then she shouldn't mind being examined by the vet.

Vaccinations

You must protect your dog against common infectious diseases by vaccination. A puppy must be vaccinated at eight weeks and again at ten weeks (or as the vet advises), and after that once a year. A vaccination is given by injection. Your dog may feel a moment's discomfort, but shouldn't feel sick or hurt afterward, though she avoid eating for a day or two. The vet will give you a certificate to prove your dog has been vaccinated and remind you when the next one is due.

Overheating

Dogs can't sweat to cool down, they can only pant, so they sometimes suffer from heat exhaustion. Never leave your dog in a car in hot weather, even with the window open.

Parasites

Parasites — often called worms — can live in a dog's intestines. Ask your vet for advice on how to treat for them. The breeder should have treated your puppy at two and five weeks, and again at eight weeks.

Fleas

De-flea your dog regularly, even if you don't think she has fleas on her. You should get a flea product from your vet, as this will be more effective than treatments sold in pet shops.

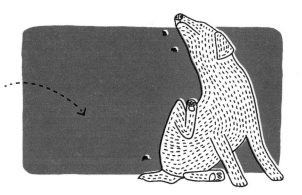

Serious illness

Most dogs live for between ten and fourteen years. One day your dog might become very sick or have an accident and could be in a lot of pain. The vet may suggest that the kindest thing to do is to euthanize her: give her an injection that would cause her to die without pain. This decision may be hard and sad to make, but it may be the kindest and most responsible thing you can do for your dog.

NEW PUPPIES

It will be fun for you if your dog has puppies, but they are a lot of work!

You will need help from an adult to look after them. If your dog is pregnant, find a book on breeding a litter to give you some detailed advice on how to take care of her and the puppies.

Choosing to have puppies

 Many people choose to have their dogs spayed or neutered: having a simple operation that means they can't have babies.

This keeps unwanted puppies from being born and provides some health benefits. An unneutered male dog may run off to look for a mate, and could get lost or run over. Pedigree dogs require a mate of the same breed.

Looking after your pregnant dog

If your dog is expecting puppies, you should take her to the vet to check that she is well and to get some advice. For the first four weeks of the pregnancy she will eat as normal, but as the puppies grow inside her you will need to increase the amount you feed her. She will also need extra nutrients, so gradually switching back to a complete puppy food is a good idea.

PUPPY FACTS

🐾 Length of pregnancy: 9 weeks

🐾 Number of puppies in a litter:
   small breeds: 1–6
   large breeds: 5–12

🐾 Puppies' eyes open at: 10 days

🐾 Weaning can begin at: 4 weeks

🐾 Puppies can leave mother at:
   8–12 weeks

🐾 Best age for a female to have
   her first puppies: 1.5 years

During and after the birth

Dogs usually give birth easily, so yours should not need help having her puppies, though you may want to stay and quietly reassure her. Watch her carefully for the first week after the birth to make sure she shows no signs of illness. Then, at about three weeks, take her to the vet with her puppies for a check-up.

For the first four weeks the puppies will need only their mother's milk, but after that you can begin to wean them onto solid food. While the mother is nursing, she will need to eat a lot, so increase the number of meals you give her. Enjoy this special time as the puppies grow and learn to explore the world!

INDEX